All About
Sir Edmund Hillary

Lew Freedman

BLUE RIVER PRESS
Indianapolis, Indiana

All About Sir Edmund Hillary
Copyright © 2016 by Lew Freedman

Published by Blue River Press
Indianapolis, Indiana
www.brpressbooks.com

Distributed by Cardinal Publishers Group
Tom Doherty Company, Inc.
www.cardinalpub.com

ISBN: 978-1-68157-087-7

Author: Lew Freedman
Series Editor: Charleen Davis
Editors: Morgan Sears and Dani McCormick
Interior Illustrator: Amber Calderon
Book Design: Dave Reed
Cover Artist: Jennifer Mujezinovic
Cover Design: David Miles

Printed in the United States of America

Contents

Edmund smiled while his teammates took his picture
after his successful Everest climb in 1953

All About
Sir Edmund Hillary

Preface

Mount Everest is the tallest mountain in the world at 29,035 feet. Its massive size straddles the countries of Nepal and China and was first studied in 1856 by the Great Trigonometric Survey of India. In 1865, the Royal Geographic Society of England established a height of 29,002 feet. In 1955, a more advanced measuring system set the height at 29,029 feet. Then in 1999 a re-measurement recorded the latest height.

In 1865, the huge mountain was named after Colonel Sir George Everest, the Surveyor General of India. Locals of the region have other names for Mount Everest. One is Chomolungma, which translates to "Goddess Mother of the Earth." Another local name is Deodungha which means "Holy Mountain".

Over the centuries, whether it was exploring the unmapped oceans, racing to see the North and South Poles, or climbing the tallest mountains on the planet, man's curiosity has led to daring explorations. The English have always wanted to explore and discover new places. They thought that Everest was "their" mountain and very much wanted to be the first people to climb it.

Mount Everest (middle) is part of the Himalayan mountain range which boasts nine of the ten tallest mountains in the world

In the early 1920s, English mountaineers tried to become the first to climb Everest. The expedition in 1924, which included George Mallory and Andrew Irvine, was the most famous. It was Mallory who uttered what is probably the most famous phrase in mountaineering history. When asked why he wanted to climb Mount Everest he said, "Because it's there." However both climbers disappeared on the mountain and what happened on their trip was a mystery.

George Mallory and Andrew Irvine attempted to climb Mt. Everest in 1924, but disappeared before reaching the top

It was not until after World War II that explorers' and mountaineers' attention fully focused on climbing the Earth's peaks that stood 26,000 feet and higher. By then it was understood that such expeditions could be very dangerous, especially attempts in the Karakoram region of India and Pakistan. Additionally, the combination of extreme cold, wind, snow, ice, and altitude could easily become deadly for the mountaineers.

There are fourteen mountains in the world that reach at least 26,300 feet high. These mountains were considered important to climb for historical and scientific reasons and various European nations' governments helped organize and pay for expeditions trying to be the first to the top. England, France, and Switzerland were among the most active European nations. The nation that reached the summits first would earn great honor and pride. The biggest prize of all was Everest since it was the tallest peak in the world.

When China took over Tibet in 1950, all access was denied to the north side of the mountain. It would not reopen to foreigners until 1979. Access to Everest from the south was controlled by the Nepalese government. By 1953, the Nepalese were willing to permit just one attempt per year.

The scale of such expeditions was tremendous, with a small group of climbers hiking miles across rugged ground to an area that led to the start of a route uphill. It took months to hike into the area that came to be called "base camp" at the bottom of Everest. Months worth of supplies were carried by teams of hundreds of porters, with these laborers generally being made up of the local Sherpa people. Sherpa translates to the word "people" and is what those who live in the mountains of Nepal call themselves.

Edmund Hillary and Tenzing Norgay, a Nepalese Sherpa, climbed Mt. Everest together as a team and became lifelong friends

It was through this combined effort of British Commonwealth mountaineers and local, native Nepalese workers that Edmund Hillary and Tenzing Norgay were pushed together by fate. By chance, they were paired together as climbing partners. At the end of May 1953, they became the first human beings to stand together on the highest point on earth.

Chapter 1
Growing Up

Born in Auckland, New Zealand on July 20, 1919, Edmund Percival Hillary was the son of Percival A. Hillary and Gertrude Clark Hillary.

Gertrude Clark Hillary, Edmund's mother, sits in the cow barn in 1920 shortly after Edmund is born

When Edmund was very young, the family moved to a more remote country area about forty miles south of Auckland called Tuakau. In Tuakau his father ran the local, weekly newspaper. The Hillary family decided to live in this area because his father was awarded land in the region for his

Percival A. Hillary, Edmund's father, was a World War I soldier, beekeeper, and newspaper editor during Edmund's childhood

military service. Edmund's father, Percival, had served during World War I, and fought in the great and long Battle of Gallipoli, which lasted from April of 1915 to January 1916.

After World War I Edmunds's father married Edmund's mother, Gertrude Clark in 1916. The family was not especially well off financially, but Edmund always found a way to play and work outdoors.

Edmund had many chances to play outside on his family's large plot of land and became an adventurous child

Edmund was the middle child. He had an older sister, June Hillary, and a younger brother, Rex Hillary. As a youngster, Edmund was shy and, initially, he was smaller than the other children. Eventually, he became slender, wiry, and strong. He grew to be 6 foot 2 inches tall. Living on seven acres of land, where his father built the house and milked a dozen cows, the Hillarys resided about a half-mile walk from the elementary school, a stroll that Edmund took barefoot.

Young Rex, June, and Edmund pose
for pictures at the family farm in 1946

Many of the other children in the area and at school were members of the Maori tribe, the native people of New Zealand. The Maori people are originally from Polynesia; there are about 750,000 of them living all around the world. By far though, the largest amount of Maori people live in New Zealand. New Zealand is estimated to have 598,000 Maori tribe members living in the country. It is believed that the large tribe migrated to New Zealand long ago, between the years 1250 and 1300, on canoes. Historically they were renowned as great warriors and experts in horticulture, the growing of plants.

There was no separation between the races and Edmund interacted with and was friends with young people from all walks of life. It may be that the nature of Hillary's rural upbringing helped him identify with the native peoples.

Edmund's family was not wealthy, but during the Great Depression of the late 1920s and 1930s, there was no shortage of food on the table because of an orchard on the family property and vegetables grown on the farm. They were capable of living off of the land and supporting themselves.

While running the local newspaper, Percival Hillary also raised bees. It was somewhat of a family enterprise with everyone chipping in to help. By the time Edmund was sixteen, working as a beekeeper was the activity, besides school, that kept him the busiest.

As beekeepers, the Hillarys raised bees in hives on the family property. While many people are fearful of bees because they can sting and inflict

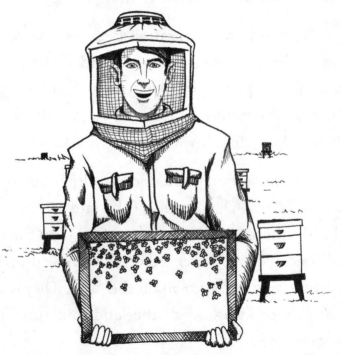

Edmund shows off his sedated bees
while wearing a traditional beekeeping suit

pain, beekeeping is an industry. A bee producer, who develops bee colonies, can sell honey, beeswax, or use the bees for pollinating crops. Some individuals raise bees just for the fun of it as a hobby, but the Hillarys did so as a job.

They would cover their bodies head-to-toe, including wearing a mesh-like mask over their faces, to avoid stings. Others may try to get by only with a mask, or veil, and gloves. Regardless of how careful beekeepers are, they are bound to be stung at one time or another.

Along with wearing the proper clothing, another method of protection that beekeepers use is spraying smoke into the beehive. Smoke calms bees down, reducing aggressive behavior.

Edmund took beekeeping seriously and he enjoyed it as well, but he was not always as obedient regarding other aspects of life. Somewhat mischievous, Edmund often broke his father's rules about misconduct and was frequently spanked as punishment. It was unclear who was more stubborn, the father or the son, but decades later Edmund definitely recalled his father's physical disciplining in the woodshed.

Edmund was a quick learner and he completed his primary school education when he was eleven, two years ahead of time. His father was ready for him to retire from school and become a farm hand, but Edmund's mother insisted he continue his education at higher levels. He was then enrolled in a school in Auckland, where he would complete his high school education. Every weekday Edmund took the train from the farm to school. The train ride to Auckland for school took two hours each way, and young Hillary spent the time as a voluminous reader. That served as bonus education, but also fueled his imagination. Hillary often dreamed of adventures in faraway places.

Auckland Grammar School is a boys' school founded in 1868 to continue education after primary school, or 8th grade

Originally—especially since his growth spurt had not happened yet—Edmund was uncomfortable in this new school that enrolled 1,200 boys. At that time, Edmund was not very coordinated and did not fit in with any sports team. He spent his free time alone reading adventure books and also dreaming of the day when he might undertake a big adventure himself. However, by the time he was fourteen years old, Edmund was growing a few inches a year and starting to approach the later peak of his height.

Edmund took to bicycle riding and then he began taking boxing lessons. With his long reach he developed a very solid left jab. He also became a sergeant in the school's military battalion, though his group spent a long time mastering their parade formations.

Edmund was able to persuade his stubborn father to allow him to join classmates on an out-of-town trip to Mount Ruapehu, where skiing would be available. He had some spending money too, from honey crop profits from beekeeping. This was Edmund's first experience with any kind of mountain besides looking at one from a distance, although his ten day journey revolved around skiing, not climbing. He loved being in the outdoors, skiing downhill, and he developed a powerful kinship with nature.

Edmund attended University of Auckland for a couple years before returning home to help his father beekeep

After completing high school in the city at Auckland, Edmund entered a university and spent two years studying. But he never felt he belonged and did not do well in school. Rather than being confined in classrooms, Edmund liked to spend time with a group that went winter hiking in the woods. Instead of spending all of his money on train tickets, he saved his change by walking five miles to the university from where he lived. The money that he saved let him enjoy walking outside every day and let him go hiking with his friends.

During the summers, Edmund spent his time working with the bees back at the farm. Percival Hillary was immersed in beekeeping. He was the founder of the New Zealand Beekeepers' Association and served as its president. Edmund dropped out of the university, and along with his brother, joined his father as full-time beekeepers. He said he liked the work because it kept him outdoors and it was good physical labor. The Hillary family had acquired over 1,600 bee hives.

That was the life that Edmund settled into and enjoyed until Germany invaded Poland in September of 1939, and World War II began. World

War II is considered the deadliest war in history; it caused between fifty million and eighty million deaths of both soldiers and civilians. There were two major battle fronts, one in Europe and one in the Pacific Ocean.

In Europe, Germany and its dictator, Adolf Hitler, who was the leader of the Nazi party, were trying to conquer more territory, triggering the War. The Nazi party enslaved many people that they though were inferior to themselves. When Germany invaded Poland, countries across the world decided that they must join forces to stop Hitler and Germany.

On the other side of the globe, in the Pacific Ocean, Japan also wanted to build its empire and they started to invade other countries. Eventually the Japanese bombed Hawaii and the United States had to join the world war to defend itself. The United States was then an ally to New Zealand among other countries.

Feeling it was his duty, Edmund applied to the Royal New Zealand Air Force, hoping to receive pilot training. As 1939 turned to 1940, the service was slow to process his application.

Edmund's desire to mountain climb was sparked during a trip to New Zealand's Southern Alps

While he had to wait to find out what his immediate future would be, Edmund took some time off from work and traveled with a friend to the Southern Alps. On the drive, the scenery left him spellbound. He loved looking at the rocky, mountainous walls, glaciers, and areas where avalanches cut through the hills. Edmund did not have any mountaineering training or experience at this point, but almost as soon as he got settled at his hotel he wanted to take a walk up the nearest hill to the snow line.

The beauty of the area attracted him, but Edmund discovered that his route was steeper and harder than he thought it would be. Climbing was more strenuous than he imagined, and it took a lot of focus, strength, and endurance. Still, he did reach the point he set as a goal and felt proud of himself for making it. That evening, at twenty years old, Hillary found his true inspiration, something that made for a turning point of his life. Two young men came into the hotel, fresh from climbing Mount Cook, New Zealand's highest peak. Edmund was so excited listening to them, and noticing the way the young women in the room seemed to admire them. He decided on the spot that he wanted to climb the closest mountain.

As enthusiastic as Edmund was, his friend's attitude was far more cautious. He agreed to go with Edmund as long as they were accompanied by a guide. The next day they set off for the mountains and ascended Mount Ollivier, a mountain that is 6,342 feet high. Mount Ollivier is part of a range of mountains called Sealy Range. It is named after another great New Zealand mountaineer, Arthur Morton Ollivier.

Mount Ollivier sat in the middle of a mountain range of taller mountains, but was Edmund's first successful summit in 1939

Edmund felt a special sense of achievement. This was the first major mountain he had ever climbed. He would go on to climb many more mountains in much more difficult conditions and ones that were more than four times the height of Mt. Ollivier, but he would always remember that first climb. He never forgot how joyful he was about the accomplishment, and would have good memories of that day for the rest of his life. The first ascent of Mount Ollivier confirmed his love of the mountains and ignited a passion for climbing which would soon lead to greatness and fame.

Chapter 2
Military Service

The entire time Hillary was climbing Mt. Ollivier he was still waiting on a response from the Royal New Zealand Air Force. While patriotic enough to take this step, he abruptly withdrew his application after he had traveled the Southern Alps and climbed Mount Ollivier with his friend. He had gained a new perspective and outlook and felt he was too much of a pacifist to fight. He took the drastic step of withdrawing his application because he realized his religious beliefs strongly conflicted with the idea of war.

As the war continued on, it took a bad turn for New Zealand. There was a threat of Japanese invasion and conquest looming over the country. With this more urgent matter, Edmund again changed his mind. The cause was just too powerful to ignore now.

He did not learn until later that his own father intervened and wrote to the authorities to say

he was performing essential work as a beekeeper involved with the honey crop and he should
not leave home for military service. It took until
1942 for the stubborn Percival Hillary to relent;
and Edmund applied to the Air Force yet again.

Edmund finally graduated the New Zealand Air Force Academy
at Delta Camp in 1944

While he waited to learn if he would be given the chance to fly, Edmund suited up with the Home Guard. As a small island nation, New Zealand was located far away from its war allies, the United States and parts of Europe. To protect itself from Japan, New Zealand created the Home Guard in 1940. The Home Guard took volunteer soldiers as young as fifteen years old. It was not the official Army of New Zealand, but was just a back-up protection against Japan. Edmund was not alone serving in the Home Guard, in fact as many as 120,000 New Zealanders volunteered. Edmund participated in military exercises on weekends and worked during the week. There was great fear in New Zealand that the Japanese enemy would take control of the entire Pacific Ocean and invade the country. In 1943, Edmund was accepted into the Royal Air Force, and in 1944, he became active in training.

During one break, Edmund became overwhelmed with the idea of climbing Mount Tapuaenuku, a 9,465 foot peak. Initially, it seemed as if a large group of flyers were going to climb the mountain together, but they were not ordered to and most of them lost interest. Edmund, fascinated with what he considered to be a beautiful summit, still wanted to go. He ended up climbing the mountain on his own, which is called a solo climb.

Although he did not have experience solo climbing, Edmund hiked to the starting point, camped overnight, cooked, and began plodding upward through deep snow. It was a slog because of the heavy nature of the snow and at one point Hillary became alarmed because he was almost struck by a large hunk of ice that ripped loose from the mountain and nearly conked him on the head.

Eventually, Edmund reached the summit, but he realized immediately that he could not linger there. If he did not hurry he would have to climb down in darkness, something which could be very risky. As it so happened, Edmund did not move quickly enough, and he became enveloped in darkness on his descent.

After fourteen hours of climbing, Edmund reached the mountain hut where he paused on his way up and spent the rest of the night resting. He began descending again at 4 a.m. and made it off the mountain safely. After walking for hours along the road, Edmund was at last picked up by a passing truck and made it back to his military camp without being late or getting into trouble.

Edmund played rugby frequently. In 2008,
the New Zealand National Rugby Union named a trophy
after him: the Hillary Shield

Around this time, Edmund joined a rugby team for seven-on-seven play. He filled out his form at six foot and two inches and 190 pounds, making him a sturdy player. Whenever he got the chance, he also set off for the mountains to climb again, almost always on his own.

Solo climbing is demanding and dangerous. It can also be fulfilling to be alone in nature and Hillary did enjoy being in the wilderness and observing the scenery. He had some close calls where having a partner would have been helpful, even once while crossing a river to approach a mountain.

Before his air force training was complete, Edmund found a couple of companions who also liked to spend their free time in the near-by mountains and he did climb with them as a group.

For the next step in military training, Edmund was transferred to a navigation class. This was in a different area of the country, but it was also near some different mountains so Edmund had new areas to explore. His favorite playground be-came Mount Egmont, a mountain of 8,261 feet in height. Once again he often climbed solo if he could not find a handy partner. Sometimes he was accompanied by others with similar enthusi-asm. One time, a party of nine climbed together.

When Edmund was awarded a ten day leave for Christmas in 1944, rather than return to the family farm, he embarked on his own idea of a fun holiday. After talking with a potential partner, he decided to tackle climbing Mount Cook. Mount Cook is 12,218 feet high and was the highest mountain in New Zealand. Mount Cook is located in the Southern Alps in the South Island of New Zealand. It actually has a total of three summits. Edmund wanted to reach the tallest of the three, High Peak.

Mount Cook was known for its large number of crevasses, which made climbing difficult and dangerous, especially alone

One of the difficulties a mountaineer faced when climbing Mount Cook was crevasse danger. Crevasses are deep openings on glaciers that sneak up on climbers if they can't see them. If someone is not paying attention, he or she can easily step in one of these large holes and disappear into the depths. Falls into crevasses can frequently be fatal and they create more of a problem for a climber on his or her own without a partner who can help pull them out if necessary.

Edmund's partner never showed up for the climb despite their prior arrangement, and once Edmund surveyed the crevasses of Cook he decided to change his own plans. The crevasses made Mount Cook too dangerous for a solo climb.

Instead, Edmund climbed some other medium-sized mountains in the area. With sunny weather, he ascended Mount Kitchener, Mount Annette, and scaled most of Mount Sealy. He made the tough decision to stop short of the summit on Sealy and turn back for his own safety. Making such a judgment call is often the wisest choice a climber makes. He recognizes that he could get hurt and chooses instead to live to climb another day.

Edmund had to change plans after his climbing partner didn't show up and instead climbed three other mountains in the Mount Cook National Park

That was the end of Edmund's mountaineering for a while. With his basic pilot training complete, he was shipped off to the Fiji Islands. It was the first time he had ever been out of his home country. Edmund found Fiji to be beautiful, but remarkably hot and uncomfortable. Here he underwent a more active phase of training, preparing for potential combat. However, in his spare time he went sailing. Edmund learned how to fly at night and navigate by the stars. Once, he flew to New Caledonia.

As he gained experience flying, sometimes Edmund and his crew were assigned to rescue ill civilians and bring them to hospitals for treatment.

Edmund enjoyed flying for the Royal New Zealand Air Force, especially on night trips where he navigated with the stars

On a break from flying, Edmund learned about the tallest mountain the area, twelve miles away, and he and a friend went after it. Their early investigation of the area was time-consuming and discouraging. The mountain was difficult to approach and they ran out of time almost before they got started.

Somewhat later, Edmund got another crack at the mountain with two other partners, unfortunately on a very rainy day. Trying to cope with challenging terrain and a narrow ledge near the summit, they stopped just short of the top because the situation seemed too dangerous. They had a tough enough time getting back to camp at all and arrived completely covered in mud.

Edmund climbed mountains wherever he went, even in the pouring rain on the tallest peak in Fiji in 1945

From Fiji, Edmund was transferred to the Solomon Islands and he was assigned search and rescue missions by air. The United States and Japan fought terrible and famous battles in the Solomon Islands, but by the time Edmund was posted there the worst of the fighting was over.

The official end of World War II was September 2, 1945. The European front had ended earlier in May, when Allied forces took back the land that Germany had conquered. In the Pacific Ocean, the war raged on until the United States decided to drop the first Atomic bombs in Hiroshima and Nagaski, Japan. These bombs forced the Japanese to surrender.

As the war ended with Japan's surrender, Edmund's flying tasks were reduced to returning personnel back to New Zealand. However, he had one scare in the Solomon Islands. On a routine local flight, Edmund and his crew were returning to their base camp when suddenly the gasoline tank broke free and a portion of the plane near the engine burst into flames. Both Edmund and his co-pilot suffered burns and bailed out as the plane crashed into the ocean and exploded.

It was a painful five hundred yard swim to shore, especially with the injuries the two pilots had. Edmund's injuries were the worst by far and his commanding officer even sent a note to his family saying that he was critically ill. It was determined that Edmund lost forty percent of his skin from the explosion and needed surgery. During his hospital stay, Edmund counted having 140 penicillin injections to fight off infection. Although originally doctors told Edmund he would have to stay in the hospital for months, he began healing quickly and was released after three weeks and allowed to return to New Zealand. The incident occurred in 1945 as World War II ended. Hillary could have become one of the last casualties if he had not found the strength to swim to shore.

The crew of Edmund's plane all survived a crash in 1945, but had to swim to shore with burns covering their bodies

Although at first he was reluctant to join the Air Force and participate in history's worst and most widespread war, Edmund recognized that the stakes were high and so engaged himself in the war and appropriately served his country. Hillary was not a hero in the manner of earning combat medals in fights, but in a circumstance that demanded courage to survive, he acted heroically.

Chapter 3
New Zealand Climbs

Edmund Hillary returned home to New Zealand and, after his body healed, he went back to work in the family beekeeping business. But he was twenty-six years old and restless. He had seen other parts of the world and he didn't know if he wanted to remain on the farm; he felt there were other places in the world to explore.

So many less fortunate than Hillary were killed during World War II, saw horrible things, or were seriously injured for life because of their wounds. Hillary was lucky enough to fight in the war near its end. He was not involved in combat. He enjoyed flying and in some ways his free time seemed almost like a vacation with time spent in sailboats and mountain climbing and soaking up the sun.

One thing Hillary was sure of, once his body was back to full strength, he wanted to spend more time mountain climbing. Hiking in the hills, climbing to the highest points, was his first real

New Zealand, Edmund's home, offered many mountains
for him to climb on its two islands

passion and priority. He liked the strenuous physical aspect of working his way up the slopes of mountains and he liked being out in nature. For Hillary, mountain climbing was the perfect activity.

Still, Edmund was a young and inexperienced climber. He had started somewhat later than others, and really had no mentor or wise instructor to guide him. Mostly he learned by doing, by hiking and climbing on his own, or reading mountaineering stories. As soon as his body was able, Hillary and a friend, Jack McBurney, went off on a two-man expedition to the area by Mount Cook.

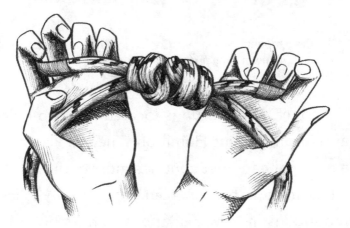

Edmund had to learn how to tie a sturdy knot,
a skill that could save his life on dangerous climbs

They climbed the same Mount Sealy which Hillary had turned back on the year before, 9,925 foot Mount Hamilton, and 10,495 foot Malte Brun. Then they undertook a greater challenge, climbing the 9,680 foot Mount De La Beche. The peaks are all in the same vicinity. Even though Mount De La Beche's summit was shorter, it ended up offering the most challenging climb.

The three mountains near Mt. Cook offered good practice on climbing in similar conditions at a lower altitude

In fact, Malte Brun is located just two miles away from Mount Hamilton. They all lie within a national park that contains most of the southern island and has nineteen of the twenty tallest mountains in New Zealand within its boundaries. Each of the mountains offered good exercise and training for climbing on snow and ice, with altitude not being a serious obstacle.

However, the climb of Mount De La Beche offered lessons. The weather turned bad on Edmund and Jack. They had to plod through rain and fog and without being able to see very far ahead they had to step around crevasses, getting a good grip with the crampons, or spikes, on their shoes. They were also hit by strong winds. One crevasse delayed them a long time. It was so wide they could not jump across. This was an occasion where it was very important that

Edmund used crampons and climbing rope to prevent himself from sliding down the steep slopes of the mountain

two climbers were traveling together and Edmund was not solo climbing. Through the use of ropes, they were able to help one another across the crevasse, avoiding the danger. As it was, they pretty much had to tip-toe carefully and pull one another to safety with the help of their climbing ropes.

While no one wants to get injured or risk their life on a climb, a close call can be educational by helping out in similar, future situations. Edmund kept climbing in his free time and even participated in many winter climbs. Typically, mountaineering in the winter is more difficult because weather extremes and sometimes storms interfere to such a degree that it is impossible to go forward. Anyone climbing in winter is bound to become tougher, stronger, and wiser.

As Edmund became immersed more into the climbing world, he made friends that had similar ambitions and interests. This meant that most of the time he could find partners to climb with instead of going solo. Edmund became pals with Harry Ayers, the man he personally ranked as the best climber in New Zealand. Edmund considered Ayers to be a legend and an expert at ice climbing. Any serious mountaineer from New Zealand had one particular goal in 1947, and Edmund reached the point where he felt it was time to conquer Mount Cook, the nation's most famous, rugged peak. The first recorded climb of Mount Cook happened in 1894. Amongst New Zealand mountaineers—and most definitely Hillary's friends and fellow climbers—it was seen as a special accomplishment, and almost an obligation to reach the top of the country's highest mountains, but especially Mount Cook, the most famous of all.

Climbing with a partner, like Harry Ayers, was always safer and, for Edmund, more enjoyable than climbing alone

Mount Cook is the centerpiece mountain in the Southern Alps and is surrounded by a national park. The official name is actually Aoraki/Mount Cook, paying tribute to English speaking residents and Maori indigenous peoples. Aoraki roughly translates in English to "Cloud Piercer." This meant the mountain's summit was sometimes seen to be higher than some clouds.

To get to Mt. Cook in 1948, Edmund had to cross a swinging bridge over Hooker River

Edmund was thrilled to climb Mount Cook in a group that included Ayers, admiring the experienced climber's instincts as they went. The team of Ayers, Sullivan, Ruth Adams, and Edmund Hillary were going to reach the summit by a route that had never been climbed before, the

South Ridge. Hillary felt a great sense of satisfaction when he stood on the summit of Mount Cook. It was very windy and that created a chill, but the view was unmatched and he soaked it in, looking far in all directions.

Hillary referred to this ascent as one fulfilling his "first major ambition" and called it "a day of triumph." He was very proud to reach the 12,349 foot summit. As someone from New Zealand it

Hillary enjoyed cross-country skiing, which helped him gain endurance for difficult climbs

meant something very special to be able to say he had visited the highest point in the country.

Listed as slightly taller when Hillary made his climb as a young man, the measurement of Mount Cook's height was changed to 12,218 feet in 2004. A rock slide and erosion were given as the reasons for the lower elevation.

Hillary mostly split his time between bee-keeping and mountain climbing. Tied in with his mountaineering were regular outings on skis. Taking off on cross-country skis was just another way to enjoy the backcountry in winter. Skiing was also good for building stamina. Hillary went on these outings for fun, but he also picked up knowledge that would serve him well.

He became an expert using an ice axe; the tool was a mountaineer's best friend. A combination of an axe and a pick, the ice axe could be employed as a walking stick for balance, for testing snow depth, or for chipping holes in otherwise smooth blocks of ice to see if stairs could be cut to aid walking. Also, if a climber took a tumble and started to roll down a hill, an ice axe could be used to stop the fall and save him from plunging over a cliff or falling into rocks.

Ice axes could save a climber's life and were used for slowing descents, carving out steps, walking sticks, and many other things

Edmund and his friend Jack McBurney took off four weeks hunting deer one winter. Another time they panned for gold, though they did not unearth very much. All of this was good preparation for a more challenging mountaineering task.

In general, Edmund's activity in the post-war years gave him a reputation and made him better known in New Zealand's mountaineering community. There is nothing a top-notch climber likes better than being part of a "first ascent," being either the climber or member of the group writing a little bit of history by going where other humans have never gone before.

Sometimes this means climbing a mountain for the very first time, or it means climbing a mountain by a new route no one has managed before. In early 1948, Hillary became part of an expedition that was going to try to climb Mount Cook by ascending over its South Ridge. Almost always, mountains are climbed for the first time by the easiest route possible. Only after someone has reached the summit do future climbers seek to find a new way to the top regardless of how hard it is.

Only one group had ever been on Mount Cook's South Ridge and it had to turn back from the summit because of bad weather. It was one of Hillary's quiet ambitions to try to climb the South Ridge. This is where his friendship with Harry Ayers and all of his stamina-building and experience gained on other New Zealand mountains paid off.

A four-person team of Edmund, Ayers, Mike Sullivan, a prominent guide, and Ruth Adams, a recognized first-rate skier, set out for the top. Traveling light, they began in good weather, but late in the day it grew cloudier and windier. At one stage, they had to use their axes to cut steps to cross an icy slope. And eventually, they had to take a break to sleep out on a rock ledge.

The team had to camp on a rocky ledge
on the side of Mt. Cook for a night

Since this was the first time anyone had climbed the South Ridge, the work of the climb also required the mountaineers to be pathfinders. They were the ones establishing the route for the future. This demanded making very careful steps because they also had to be able to get back down the mountain in case they could not go over the top and descend by an established route. Luckily, this did not happen.

Mount Cook's South Ridge had yet to be conquered until Ayer's team, which Edmund was on, did so in 1948

Near the very top, the route flattened out a little bit and led them to the summit. They had done it! In a surprising twist, as the quartet gazed around admiring the spectacular scenic views, they saw flashing lights. Some 9,000 feet lower, people had been able to spot them through telescopes and, by holding mirrors up to the sunlight, they were able to flash a message of congratulations.

It is often said in mountaineering that more injuries and deaths occur on the way down from mountains than on the way up. Once climbers have given their all to reach the summit, they tend to relax and that can lead to problems. Climbers are also often rushed for time on descents since it took them most of the day to reach the summit. They then increase their speed, which is more dangerous. Furthermore, when mountaineers climb downward, they cannot see footholds as easily so their footing is less stable. Unfortunately, that very thing happened on the way down from Mount Cook.

Shockingly, as Ruth Adams was following Mike Sullivan on an icy spot, the rope broke and within seconds she fell and slid down a steep slope, over an ice wall, and only stopped when she crashed into a large rock. When Hillary and Ayers reached

Adams she was unconscious, bleeding, and clearly suffering from broken bones. Their happy descent immediately turned into a rescue mission.

Ayers and Sullivan left to get help and Hillary stayed with the moaning Adams. At last, she regained consciousness and Hillary gave her aspirin. Hillary dug an ice cave to protect them from the wind and carried Adams into it. Sullivan returned late with a sleeping bag for Adams and the trio shared hot drinks. The next morning a small plane flew overhead and dropped supplies.

Hillary built an ice cave to protect the injured Ruth until help could arrive

Much later that next day, a team of guides who were accompanied by a doctor reached them and a plan unfolded to get Adams to a hospital. More rescuers arrived and eventually Adams was strapped onto a stretcher. It took three more days of careful descending over ice and snow to reach the bottom of Mount Cook. Adams was flown to Christchurch and recovered from her injuries. Hillary had not only been part of a significant first ascent, but played an important role in saving another person's life.

Nearly half a century later, New Zealand officials chose to honor Edmund by renaming a point on Mount Cook after him. Additionally a museum was built near the mountain named "The Sir Edmund Hillary Alpine Centre" and a statue of Edmund, rope in hand, is located outside the front entrance.

Chapter 4
Himalayan Expeditions

In 1950, when his sister June got married in England, Edmund traveled to Europe for the first time and afterwards drove his parents around sightseeing through several countries. Then he met two friends from New Zealand and made his first European mountain climbs in Austria and Switzerland. From the Southern Alps to the European Alps, Edmund was checking out the mountains.

The Swiss Alps offered a new and exciting challenge for Edmund in 1950

Edmund arrived in Switzerland with particular excitement. He knew that the Swiss had been amongst the world's greatest pioneers in mountaineering, so it felt special to be there. Edmund climbed some peaks over 11,000 feet tall. When one friend departed for home, Edmund and the other climber continued bagging summits. However, at one point Edmund's friend was standing on a chunk of snow that protruded from a slope only to have it collapse under him. It took some effort to haul him back to safe ground by rope. That incident showed how scary close calls can happen in the mountains.

Hillary not only had a grand time being out in the European mountains, he was adding to his level of mountaineering expertise. The more he did, the more he improved his reputation, and before he left Europe he received an intriguing letter from a good friend in the New Zealand climbing community. The letter from George Lowe informed Edmund that a New Zealand expedition was being formed for the Himalayas for 1951. The group was either going to try to climb

Mount Everest or Kangchenjunga, the third tallest mountain in the world at 28,169 feet.

Edmund was excited to receive a letter from his friend George Lowe inviting him to join a Himalayan expedition in 1951

Lowe's letter invited Hillary to join the team if he wished. It was an exciting opportunity and he was glad to be part of it. However, as months passed, the expedition ran into many problems. The first was getting a climbing permit. Second was fundraising. Some members quit and others joined. The goal was scaled down. Instead of thinking so big, the team set its eyes on ascending 23,760 foot Mukut Parbat, which had never been climbed.

The expedition made its way to Madras in India, where the climbers hopped on a train that carried them slowly through the country. They chugged through Calcutta, across the Ganges River, enduring temperatures of 113 degrees, and finally rode a bus for the last fifty-eight miles. When Hillary first got a clear view of the region's huge mountains, he was almost overcome with emotion because they were so impressive and amazingly beautiful.

Edmund, John Hunt, and Tenzing Norgay discuss a route up Mount Everest's dangerous southern slope in 1953

For the first time, Hillary met Sherpa people. Four porters were assigned to work with the New Zealand group. Right from the beginning, Edmund was impressed with the Sherpas' strong work ethic and always-cheerful outlook. The Sherpas brought a good attitude to the team. Supplies were packed and a fifty mile bus ride followed. The final stage of the journey to the mountains was a ten day, one hundred mile march while carrying provisions. Some of the loads on a porter's back weighed up to seventy pounds.

Surrounded by the Himalayan giants, the group began climbing on mountains which would be the biggest around anywhere else in the world, but were smaller ones in this neighborhood. Difficult weather conditions slowed ascents, but slogging through deep snow the group did climb a 20,330 foot mountain—Hillary's first of that height—that was just one of many local peaks.

Once climbing of Mukut Parbat began in a serious way, the mountaineers had to thread their way through rocks and push hard through deep snow, all of which made progress slow. A high camp was established at above 21,000 feet and when the weather was good, team members went off to climb nearby tall peaks. Despite harsh cold, avalanches, and heavy snow interrupting them, their patience paid off. Half of the group reached the summit while the other half, including Edmund, waited below. The summit was the final thing before going home after the months-long adventure.

Right after that, Edmund was included on another trip in the Himalayas. This trip was designed

The team climbed through heavy snow and wore very warm, insulating clothes to try to keep out the cold Himalayan wind

by the British to scout the best possible route to finally succeed at climbing Mount Everest. The journey's leader was famed English mountaineer Eric Shipton. New Zealand authorities asked if he would take Hillary and Earle Riddiford.

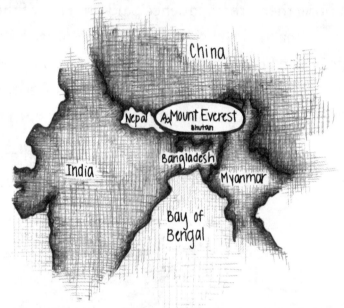

Mount Everest was the jewel of the Himalayan mountains, which formed the border for five countries

Shipton had already turned down many applicants. He had fond memories, though, of another long-ago expedition that brought him a friendship with someone from New Zealand, so he said okay. If Shipton had declined to take

Hillary on this trip, he likely would never have been selected to be part of the later Everest climb that made him famous.

The 1951 Shipton expedition was ahead of Hillary and Riddiford when they wrapped up their own trip to Mukut Parbat and they had to move fast to catch up. At that time Shipton was a hero to Hillary. He had read all of Shipton's books and would have been happy enough just to meet him. But here he was traveling with him on an important mission.

Hiking into what became Everest base camp from the village of Namche Bazaar, Hillary caught his first glimpse of the special group of mountains that emerge from the ground there and seemingly touch the sky. Mount Everest and two other great peaks, Nuptse and Lhotse (also among Earth's tallest) suddenly appeared on the horizon. Often hikers and climbers say the sight takes their breath away because it is so beautiful and majestic.

The goal of Eric Shipton's trip was to find out if Mount Everest could best be climbed from the south side of its magnificent walls. Before 1950, most had tried approaching the big mountain from the north. In the 1920s, though, famed climbers George Mallory and Andrew Irvine, who died trying to reach the summit, had investigated some of the major difficulties Everest presented to humans seeking to climb up its slopes.

After George Mallory and Andrew Irvine disappeared on the mountain, Nepal was cautious about granting permits to climb it

The most dangerous terrain on Mount Everest is called the Khumbu Icefall. The icefall is located only a short distance above base camp. The icefall often has snow and ice avalanches that fall rapidly down the mountainside. The ground is always shifting and moving, opening new crevasses and changing footing from one minute to the next. There is no way around the icefall from the south. All of the food, tents, and equipment, which are needed to climb higher, had to be carried through the unpredictable icefall.

Climbing teams always use ropes for safety and often install rope or aluminum ladders to cross extra wide crevasses or to help on very steep stretches. All of these would be needed.

While climbing, the team installed rope ladders to help them cross large crevasses in the ice more safely

It was the Khumbu Icefall that Shipton and his men studied very carefully. This was a huge obstacle to any successful climb of Everest. But above the icefall, at about 20,000 feet, they also studied the area that Mallory had named the Western Cwm. Until Shipton's scouting mission, it was believed that there was no route to the top above the icefall. Shipton's team, with Hillary on it, discovered this was not true, that in fact climbing improved above the icefall. This was a very important piece of news. It also was laying the groundwork for an Everest climb.

Climbing Cho Oyu was no small task and required careful planning, especially since it had never been climbed before

Nepal was stingy with its climbing permits, however, and the British could not obtain one to put this knowledge to use before 1953. But a permit was granted for them to try climbing Cho Oyu, the sixth tallest mountain in the world at 26,906 feet.

Cho Oyu had not yet been climbed when Shipton led the group into the area. The climbers again faced avalanche danger and Shipton received a report that some Chinese troops were nearby.

Once again, Shipton was team leader and Hillary, Riddiford, and George Lowe were all selected to represent New Zealand. Each had shown he had the right stuff based on the strength and good judgment they displayed on previous trips to the Himalayas.

Shipton always operated with the belief that it was a good thing to explore any new country while on these mountaineering expeditions, and he did not always plot the straightest route to a key mountain objective. So the party did look at new areas, but on Cho Oyu everyone was blasted by consistently harsh weather that held them back. Hillary was in tip-top shape and he and Lowe took some detours to the summit on four 20,000 foot mountains. Those were bonus accomplishments, but the group never came close to making a successful ascent of Cho Oyu. The bad weather and report of Chinese troops contributed to backing down from the climb before it could be finished.

The mountain was finally successfully climbed in 1954 by an Austrian team accompanied by one Nepalese Sherpa.

Although neither the Everest reconnaissance team, nor the Cho Oyu climbing groups achieved a major summit, Hillary gained very important experience climbing to the top on other 20,000 foot tall mountains.

Meanwhile, a team of mountaineers from Switzerland was granted the season's only permit to climb Mount Everest. While still in the Himalayas, the British team heard that the Swiss had placed seven people on Everest's summit. Shipton, Hillary and the others worried that

Swiss competitors would claim the big prize that they had chased for so long.

Tenzing Norgay made a name for himself in mountain climbing with Raymond Lambert's Mt. Everest attempt in 1952, falling just short of the summit

News of the Swiss team proved to be a false rumor. Switzerland's premier climber, Raymond Lambert, had reached the height of 28,000 feet before altitude and weather turned him back. He was climbing with a Sherpa named Tenzing Norgay at the time. In 1952, Norgay and Hillary were strangers to one another. Soon their names would be linked together forever.

Chapter 5

Conquering Everest

As the 1950s unfolded, explorers had been attempting to conquer the 26,000 foot peaks of the Himalayas for thirty years without success. These mountains were the most significant places on the planet where no man had stood. Climbing Mount Everest, or one of the thirteen other similar major mountains, was considered to be the last great challenge on earth.

Finally, in 1950, a team organized by the French Alpine Club climbed 26,545 foot Annapurna. Annapurna is the tenth highest mountain in the world and the peaks on this mountain are often regarded as some of the most dangerous climbs in the world. This remains a famous feat in mountaineering. The grandest prize in the exploration world, however, was to reach the summit of Mount Everest. This was the journey Edmund Hillary signed up for in early 1953.

A British Army officer named John Hunt was assigned as leader for the expedition, chosen by the English Himalayan Committee backing the plans for the climb. The group crossed the oceans and entered the mountains on April 12, establishing a base camp gazing up at Everest's 29,035 foot summit.

Base camp was set up close to the bottom of Mt. Everest with food, tents, and supplies on April 12, 1953

Some 362 porters carried more than 10,000 pounds of supplies to base camp for thirteen British climbers, some of whom also had additional tasks as doctors or cameramen to record the scene. Edmund Hillary had no other duties beyond climbing. In addition, the team was supplemented by Nepalese Sherpas who would both climb and carry equipment higher on the peak. Tenzing Norgay was one of these men.

The porters wore large backpacks, some weighing more than seventy pounds, to transport all of their supplies up the mountain

Aside from the threat of wintry storms at any time of the year, mountains like Everest are permanently covered with snow and ice. Also, the high altitude means that the air is very thin to breathe. All of the early Himalayan expeditions, and most of them today, expect climbers to carry and use oxygen bottles to compensate for the thin, unbreathable air.

Due to severe weather and thinner air high up
on the mountain, the climbers carried portable oxygen tanks
to make sure that they could breathe

This climb was very much like the Olympic games. While athletes qualify and compete on their own, they are representing their home country. From the 19th century on, when the British surveyed Mount Everest, there had been a special interest in this mountain. It meant more to the people of Great Britain for their own climbers to scale Everest than it would have meant if Englishmen had first climbed Annapurna. Everyone going into the trip felt a certain amount of pressure to succeed. That was partly because English teams had gone to the mountain so many times before, and partly because the climbers did not know when they would ever return for a second

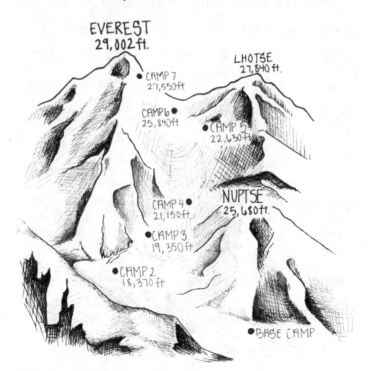

Multiple camps were made as the team went up Mt. Everest so that the climbers could get used to the changes in altitude

chance if they failed. France held the only Nepalese Everest permit for 1954 and Switzerland had the only permit for 1955.

The world's biggest mountains are climbed in stages. The human body must adapt to the high altitude gradually. Even the strongest of climbers must take time to get used to breathing the thinner air. The pattern is for groups of climbers to go upward carrying tents, food, water, and other equipment and set up a new camp. Days are spent at such a camp to rest and adjust to the altitude and air. Then the process is repeated, going higher and higher on the mountain. On Everest there is a Camp I, Camp II, Camp III,

Tenzing, Edmund and Hunt help set up camp for the night as the team regroups to sleep and gather supplies

Camp IV, Camp V, and maybe a Camp VI or VII. Each camp brings the climbers closer and closer to the top.

As they progressed, Edmund, Tenzing, and other climbers took turns ferrying supplies to the high camps, often battling high winds, temperatures far below zero, and sometimes snow. This was very hard work. When the highest camp was established, it was up to team leader John Hunt to decide who in his group looked like the strongest climbers, who looked too tired to go up right away, and which men should be paired together.

Wilford Noyce and Annullu, a Sherpa known only by one name, together reached the South Col at nearly 26,000 feet, where the route splits to ascend either to Everest's summit, or to the summit of Lhote, the fourth highest mountain in the world. With eleven British climbers at the South Col, Hunt chose the duo of Charles Evans and Tom Bourdillon to make the first try for the summit, leaving on May 26. The duo got above 28,000 feet, but turned back because they were too exhausted.

The next team consisted of Edmund and Tenzing. Before the expedition began, the men had never met, but they became friendly on the trip and had respect for one another's abilities.

Edmund and Tenzing were the second team to attempt the summit. The first team ran out of oxygen 330 feet from the top

When chosen for the expedition in late 1952, Tenzing had given his age as thirty-eight, but he did not really know. He had no birth certificate, so it was a guess. Tenzing was quite experienced on the mountain, however. He was with Swiss climber Raymond Lambert above 28,000 feet on Everest the year before, so Hillary knew Tenzing by reputation, at least. Exceptionally strong at altitude, Norgay's nickname was "Tiger of the Snows."

Hillary and Tenzing had developed a strong working partnership on the mountain during the early stages of the climb while carrying supplies. As the two men climbed together, bad weather, snow and wind slowed them and they were forced to spend two days in place at the 25,900 foot South Col camp.

This was a turning point. Staying up so high in thin oxygen for too long is dangerous to mountaineers' health and if Hillary and Tenzing had been forced to remain in place much longer they would have had to retreat and therefore lose their chance at the summit.

Often forgotten on historic climbs like this one is the help of support teams and the lead climbers were dramatically aided by George Lowe,

Alfred Gregory, and Ang Nyima. Still, Hillary and Tenzing had to set up a tent at 27,900 feet the day before their summit try.

During the late days of May, the temperature high on the mountain was extremely cold. It often dropped to negative twenty-five degrees or so. When Edmund and Tenzing awoke in their tent very early in the morning on May 29, they had to thaw out frozen boots over a portable stove.

Edmund's tent was small to conserve heat and make it lighter to carry

The twosome left camp at 6:30 a.m. in the second try for the summit. There was no clearcut route and they had to experiment. Relying on their trusty ice axes, Hillary and Norgay probed the ground ahead to avoid crevasses and sometimes pushed through deep snow which meant slow going. As they stepped, the men helped their breathing by inhaling from oxygen bottles. They traveled roped together at all times, weaving around snow covered boulders as the path narrowed.

To their surprise, as they drew closer to the summit, Hillary and Norgay were confronted by a forty foot wall of rock that at first seemed impossible to overcome. They were so close to the top of the world, but it was not to be a straight walk. Hillary looked over the problem and then called upon his experience in New Zealand climbing over rocks. He found a way past the obstacle. Later, this area was named "The Hillary Step." Once above those exposed rocks, Edmund and Tenzing had a three hundred foot stroll to the actual summit.

They had done it! For the first time in history men stood upon the highest point on earth.

It was about 11:30 in the morning. Hillary and Norgay shook hands and hugged one another in celebration. But it was viciously cold and they did not stay long at the summit—only fifteen minutes—the vast and impressively beautiful view tempting, but not overpowering enough to make them risk their lives by staying longer. Hillary snapped a picture of Norgay. Tenzing was completely bundled up with an oxygen mask covering his face, holding up an ice axe with flags of their countries tied onto it.

Tenzing held up the flags of both Nepal and New Zealand at the top of Mt. Everest while Edmund photographed him

Edmund and Tenzing ran their bottles out of oxygen, but picked up leftovers discarded by Evans and Bordillon to help them as they made their way downward. They had to focus just as much on the descent as they did on the ascent to ensure their safety after such an exhausting climb.

Team leader Hunt and other climbers had arranged for a basic signal to get information. As seen by Hunt through binoculars, if sleeping bags were set up in a particular pattern up high he would know of the climbers' success. But it got dark too early and Hunt went to bed not knowing the outcome.

It was not until a group of a half dozen men came into sight of Hunt's camp that he learned the truth. It was George Lowe, raising his ice axe and pointing to the summit, who provided the first news. First to greet them, and to learn that Everest had been climbed, was indeed Lowe, Hillary's old friend. He brought them hot soup. That night terrible weather blew in, eliminating the chance for anyone else to try for the summit.

Hunt was nearly overcome with excitement and emotions as he met the men one by one. As Hillary and Norgay told the story, a famed British journalist who had accompanied the team took notes. He immediately departed, racing to get the news out to the world.

A journalist traveling with the team hurriedly published the story, letting the world know that Mt. Everest had been conquered

Englishmen and other members of the British Empire long had been fascinated with Mount Everest. The attempt to scale the mountain by George Mallory and Sandy Irvine in the 1920s was an avidly followed adventure.

Becoming the first to ascend the world's tall-est peak had become a national obsession. Al-though Edmund Hillary was an adventurer first, and from New Zealand, his and Tenzing Norgay's triumph belonged to all of the British Empire.

The timing of the achievement could not have been better for England since only days after the men reached the summit, the British monarchy was installing a new queen on the throne. Cor-onation Day for Queen Elizabeth II was set for June 2.

Those remaining on Everest's slopes or at base camp understood that Hillary and Tenz-ing's accomplishment would be greeted with resounding enthusiasm in England at the same time the country was celebrating the crowning of Elizabeth. England was already throwing one of the biggest parties in its history. Finding out the British team had succeeded added even more national pride to the festivities.

In the modern world, technology has im-proved so much that people on the summit or at base camp can telephone halfway around the world to inform loved ones about a success-ful climb. In 1953, expedition leader John Hunt had to employ runners to retreat over the rugged terrain and return to Kathmandu to get the word out.

Queen Elizabeth II was coronated just after the Everest expedition and celebrated their success by giving them Coronation Medals engraved with "Mount Everest Expedition"

As the coronation of Queen Elizabeth II was being completed, the news flashed from Nepal that the British team had made it to the top. Already London was braced for a monumental party. A massive crowd gathered near Westminster Abbey, the official church of England's coronations, and people sang and rejoiced.

Queen Elizabeth II came up with the idea of linking the two special events together for the climbers who were thousands of miles away on the date of her coronation. She suggested that fourteen members of the expedition be awarded Coronation medals with the words: "Mount Everest Expedition."

Chapter 6
Celebrating the Ascent

Despite the effort in huffing and puffing their way to the top of the mountain, and the strain of climbing down, Edmund Hillary and Tenzing Norgay were well aware that everyone in the world was going to be interested in what they had done. They expected to be asked which one of them had actually been the first person to step on the summit. Neither wanted the joint achievement to be altered by people who were not there.

Tenzing and Edmund rest at camp on
their way up the mountain in 1953

They had worked very closely together, alternately taking lead steps, always helping one another. The truth was that one could not have achieved it without the other, without their teammate. It was a completely joint effort. So they agreed to tell everyone that they reached the summit simultaneously and they stuck to that story. Expedition leader John Hunt supported this thought by stating, "They reached it together, as a team."

The only summit photograph is of Tenzing because he didn't know how to use the camera to take pictures of Hillary. Questions certainly bombarded the two men and made-up stories were discussed about how one had to drag the other to the top. Tenzing called them nonsense and soon after the climb he signed a statement reading, "We reached the summit almost together."

Hillary and Norgay went up the mountain together as men and they came down the mountain together as heroes. Among the British climbers and the Sherpas on the mountain, they were immediately hailed and congratulated and treated as stars—together, as they both had wished. While both men were accomplished climbers and they knew that a certain celebrity would follow anyone who became the first at the top of Everest, they probably did not imagine the scope and size of the attention and honors that would be showered on them.

Tenzing waves a Union Jack as Hunt, he, and Edmund arrive in London to celebrate the successful climb

Their newfound fame caught up to them right away, even as the climbing party retraced its steps from Everest base camp through the surrounding hills and villages. Almost magically people turned up along the trail to greet and treat them with affection and applause. There seemed to be a special appreciation that Tenzing—one of their own—was one of the heroes.

Tenzing Norgay's name at birth in Tibet was Namgyal Wangdi. After his family moved to Nepal in his youth, his name was changed at the suggestion of a Buddhist Lama, or teacher. He did briefly go to a monastery, which is a quiet place to study to become a monk, but did not believe it was his calling. A monk is a religious figure in the Eastern practice of Buddhism.

Tenzing attended Tengboche Monastery at the base of Mt. Everest before deciding he didn't want to be a monk

Tenzing did not know his actual birth date, but only knew it was in May at the time when crops were being planted. After the ascent of Everest he chose in the future to celebrate his birthday on May 29, the glorious day of the ascent.

Tenzing was dark-haired, with a brilliant smile, almost a whole head shorter than Hillary, with darker skin. By the time he was around eighteen years old, Tenzing had moved to Darjeeling in India, where Sherpa climbers and porters congregated to obtain work. In 1935 he worked for Eric Shipton and Tenzing became well-known in the mountaineering fraternity after starting as a high-altitude porter on three British expeditions.

After the Everest party emerged from the mountains, Tenzing received the George Medal from Queen Elizabeth II. The George Medal rewards acts of bravery by civilians, not soldiers, and one side of the round medal is a picture of St. George slaying a dragon. Hillary and Hunt were both granted knighthoods, thus earning the title of "Sir." Hillary, Hunt, and Norgay all also received a Queen Elizabeth II Coronation

Medal. They could not be there since they were busy thousands of miles away, but they had definitely been honored by the recognition.

The King of Nepal honored Tenzing and Edmund with the Order of Gorkha Daksina Bahu, or Right Arm of the Soldier, First Class medals

Before Tenzing even got home, he had received a congratulatory message from the famed English statesman Sir Winston Churchill and many, many more followed from faraway and nearby places. The freshest hero in his own country, Tenzing was nearly overwhelmed by the crowds of people who wanted to see him and talk to him. Fans yelled, "Tenzing zindabad!" at him. That meant, "Long live Tenzing!"

Tenzing had asked someone to wire his family to let his wife and children know what had happened and to meet him in Kathmandu. The wire never got through. He never figured out why, but when the climbing party got within three miles of the Nepalese capital he was reunited with his family.

Tenzing's conquest of Mt. Everest gave Nepal's newly forming democracy something to be proud of

Mobs of people filled the streets and Tenzing, Hillary, Hunt, and others were loaded onto vehicles that Tenzing called chariots and Hillary referred to as jeeps. They were thrust into an unplanned parade. People threw colored powder in the air, as well as coins. As they moved along, Norgay held his hands together in a prayerful manner, using the Hindu method of saying hello and thanks.

Norgay was disappointed that amidst the wildness of his reception Hillary and Hunt were sometimes overlooked. But Tenzing was "The Man" in these parts. People saw him there as a native son who had accomplished something spectacular when so many before had failed. He proudly represented his country of Nepal.

When Hillary was notified by mail of his knighthood, he thought at first it was a joke. He also had never liked titles and his next thought was that he was going to have to buy new clothes and dress up more often. It was not a joke, but reality, and over the long run, to his relief, being called "Sir" did not require Hillary to dress fancy too often.

Upon landing in London, Hillary and the rest of the expedition were greeted by Eric Shipton and then whisked into the big city. For weeks straight, Hillary was the toast of the town, the featured guest at parties, lunches and dinners, at Buckingham Palace, and at an official state banquet. However, the actual ceremony of Hillary's knighthood, was not a big public affair. It was carried out by Queen Elizabeth II in a small ceremony involving members of the Everest expedition and the royal family.

Queen Elizabeth II knighted both Hunt and Hillary in a private ceremony, adding "Sir" to both of their names

Hillary called it "an amazing month" and a series of such highlights and activities that he was sure would never be repeated in his life. It was not until August that he returned to New Zealand to visit family. That was only a temporary break from public activities, however. In 1953, television was still a relatively new phenomenon, and a popular way for the public to learn about adventures like this one, which had taken place in a remote part of the globe, was to attend lectures.

Hillary took time out to get married to Louise Mary Rose in September of 1953. She was a musician he had known for many years. Louise Mary Rose was a good viola player and she greatly admired Edmund and all of his accomplishments. Rather than simply tell his stories to the bees his family raised, Hillary decided to begin lecturing about them. The newlyweds embarked on a tour with Hillary talking their way from town to town. He was lecturing and telling anyone who wanted to hear about climbing the tallest mountain on Earth.

To some extent, Edmund Hillary spent the rest of his life telling that same story of the first climb of Mount Everest. That episode made him world famous and, while he remained an adventurer and became a generous benefactor of charities, nothing he did could quite match the accomplishment of his Everest ascent.

Taking a moment away from the celebrations, Edmund married Louise Mary Rose in September 1953

Chapter 7
New Adventures

Out of their shared adventure and accomplishment, Edmund Hillary and Tenzing Norgay not only shared a deep friendship for the rest of their lives, but their names have forever been tied together in mountain climbing history. Their fame greatly affected the direction of the rest of their lives. In some ways they both became citizens of the world.

In 1954, Tenzing became the Director of Field Training at the new Himalayan Mountaineering Institute and, in 1978, he opened Tenzing Norgay Adventures. In the 2000s, one of Tenzing's sons, Jamling Tenzing Norgay, began running the company. Jamling, one of at least fifteen members of the Norgay clan to climb Mount Everest, wrote a book called *Touching My Father's Soul*, about Tenzing's life and his influence on Sherpa people.

Sometime after the Everest climb, Norgay revealed that it was Hillary who actually took the first step onto the summit, just ahead of him. When Norgay died of a cerebral hemorrhage in 1986 he was cremated. His ashes were spread at the Himalayan Mountaineering Institute.

In the years following his climb of Mount Everest, Hillary continued his adventurous life. Between 1956 and 1965, Hillary climbed ten more mountains in the Himalayas. But most immediately in the mid-1950s, he formed a partnership with

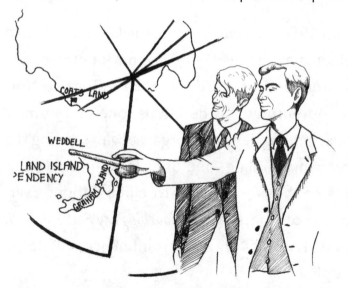

Always seeking adventure, Edmund began planning a trip to the South Pole with explorer Vivian Fuchs

explorer Vivian Fuchs and their efforts led to a creative way to reach the South Pole.

It had been nearly a half century since anyone had reached the South Pole overland, or since the original explorers Roald Amundsen (in 1911) and Robert Falcon Scott (in 1912). No one repeated an overland journey without the help of airplanes until 1981. The extreme weather of Antarctica has always limited the amount of travel and exploration on that snow-swept continent.

Spread out between 1955 and 1958, the expedition began under team leader Fuchs, who was later knighted. The team drove motorized and modified Ferguson tractors across Antarctica as part of the Commonwealth Trans-Antarctic Expedition. Employing treads like tanks used instead of wheels, the vehicles made a slow crossing of the entire continent. Small airplanes were employed for dropping supplies ahead for the Fuchs-Hillary expedition.

Ferguson tractors helped the men cover larger distances
across the snow and ice quickly and safely

Much later, in 1977, Hillary was the leader of a jet boat expedition on the Ganges River, running to its source. The 1,500 mile journey took his team from the Bay of Bengal through India and, as long as they were in the area, into the mountains at the end of the trip. There they climbed 18,000 foot peak Nar Parbut. The expedition was called "Ocean to Sky." The journey was filmed as they went, exploring the history, culture, and religion of the areas, and both a book and movie illustrated the adventure.

Edmund wrote a book in 1977 about his adventures in India traveling the Ganges River and climbing Nar Parbut

In 1985, Hillary became the first person to climb Everest and reach both the North Pole and the South Pole when he flew to the North Pole with American astronaut Neil Armstrong. Also, for three years in the 1980s, Hillary entered an entirely different career path, being sent to India as ambassador from New Zealand.

As New Zealand's ambassador to India, Edmund and his family moved there in the 1980s

While clearly the most significant honor, knighthood was hardly the end of the honors accorded to Edmund after the Mount Everest ascent. Recognition came in other ways, including becoming a recipient of the Order of New Zealand, Knight Companion of The Most Noble Order of the Garter, the Padma Vibhushan Award

Edmund, a national hero, began being featured on
New Zealand's five dollar bill in 1990

from India, the Commander's Cross of the Order of Merit of the Republic of Poland, the Polar Medal from England, and the Order of Gorkha Dakshina Bahu First Class from Nepal.

In 1990, a picture of young Hillary, as he looked when he climbed Everest, began appearing on New Zealand's five dollar bills. Sir Edmund, who always remained modest, said he did not deserve such acclaim even though he owned a very impressive trophy case. As part of the festivities surrounding the 50th anniversary of the Everest first, Peter Hillary and Jamling Tenzing Norgay climbed the mountain together as tribute to both of their fathers in 2002 while National Geographic filmed them.

Peter Hillary, Jamling Tenzing Norgay, and Brent Bishop, the son of an American mountaineer, climbed Mt. Everest together to honor their fathers' legacies in 2002

Another honor, much bigger than a personal trophy display, was afforded Hillary in 2003. A seven-and-a-half-foot tall statue of Hillary was erected outside The Hermitage Hotel near Mount Cook. It was titled "Sir Ed." Also in 2003, Hillary did receive a recognition that was dear to him. To mark the 50th anniversary of the first climb of Mount Everest, the Government of Nepal bestowed honorary citizenship on him. Hillary became the first foreigner to attain that honor. A set of postage stamps was even issued featuring Hillary in 2008.

His personal life was filled with events too. After Hillary married Louise Mary Rose in 1953, she gave birth to three children, Peter, who also became an adventurer, Sarah, and Belinda. The biggest tragedy of Hillary's life occurred in 1975, when his wife and daughter Belinda were killed in the crash of a small plane. Hillary married for a second time, to June Mulgrew in 1989.

Fourteen years after his first wife's death,
Edmund married June Mulgrew

One reason Edmund continued to collect honors as he aged was the generous way he led his life. He never let fame spoil him and was always a giving man who used his celebrity to help others. One of the two major organizations to which he devoted time, effort, and money was "The Sir Edmund Hillary Outdoor Pursuits Centre" in New Zealand. Hillary was also forever grateful to Nepal, the Sherpa people, and the friends he made on Himalayan expeditions, but was dismayed by the level of poverty he saw all around him on visits. As a result, when he was financially able, Hillary created The Himalayan Trust in 1960, and spent decades working to help the Sherpa people build schools, bridges, and hospitals. It was that continuing connection and generosity that earned him honorary citizenship to Nepal as much as his climbing expertise. He was given the title of *Burra Sahib* or "Big at Heart."

Listening to appeals for help, Hillary evaluated the requests and when he saw a need, he oversaw the construction of the schools and hospitals, visited to make sure the work was done properly, and aided in the selection of Sherpa leaders to run the operations after they opened. Of all the foreign mountaineers who came to Nepal to climb Mount Everest and others of the world's tallest mountains, no one has given back to the country more than Hillary did.

Sir Edmund Hillary was in a hospital in Auckland, New Zealand when he died of heart failure on January 11, 2008. He was eighty-eight years old and had been world famous for nearly fifty-five years. Although Hillary lived with fame, he never thought of himself as anything beyond a normal man. When he looked into the mirror he did not see someone whom he believed was a super athlete or super hero, he saw an average man. Once, he said, "You don't have to be a hero to accomplish great things—to compete. You can just be an ordinary chap, sufficiently motivated to reach challenging goals. People do not decide to become extraordinary. They decide to accomplish extraordinary things."

Hillary sought to inspire others to achieve the best that they could, no matter if they liked

Edmund continued to speak about his Everest adventure and help the Sherpa people until he died in 2008 at the age of 88

climbing or another activity. His life and legacy are an inspiration to all. On the day of his death, his home country, New Zealand, lowered their flags to half-mast, an action taken to honor the great things he had done with his life.

Select Quotes from
Sir Edmund Hillary

"The whole world around us lay spread out like a giant relief map. I am a lucky man. I have had a dream and it has come true, and that is not a thing that happens often to men."
   – *Edmund's thoughts upon climbing Mount Everest*

"I have never regarded myself as a hero, but Tenzing undoubtedly was."
   – *Edmund's opinion of his climbing partner*

"It's not the mountain we conquer, but ourselves."
   – *Edmund's insight on why we climb*

"If you only do what others have already done, you will only feel what others have already felt. However, if you choose to achieve something that no one has ever done, then you will have a satisfaction that no one else has ever had."
   – *Edmund's approach to climbing*

"I have been seriously afraid at times, but I have used my fear as a stimulating factor rather than allowing it to paralyze me."
   – *Edmund reflecting on his adventures*

Sir Edmund Hillary Timeline

1919 July 20   Born Auckland, New Zealand

1920   Family moves south to Tuakua

1924   Enters school

1930   Completes primary school

1935   Skis on Mount Ruapehu

1940   Climbs first mountain, 6,342-foot Mount Ollivier in New Zealand's Southern Alps

1943   Joins Royal New Zealand Air Force during World War II

1948 January 30   Along with others, climbs 12,316-foot Mount Cook, New Zealand's tallest mountain

1951   Part of British reconnaissance journey to Mount Everest

1952   Part of British unsuccessful attempt to climb Cho Oyu, at 26,906 feet the sixth tallest mountain in the world

1953 May 29   With Tenzing Norgay, first to summit 29,035 foot Mount Everest as part of a British expedition

1953 June 6   Appointed Knight Commander of the Order of the British Empire by Queen Elizabeth II.

1953   Marries Louise Mary Rose (deceased 1975)

1955-1958   Member of expedition completing first overland crossing of Antarctica.

1958 January 4   Reaches South Pole

1960   Founds the Himalayan Trust to benefit the people of Nepal

World Timeline

1919 January 18   World War I Peace Congress opens in Versailles, France

1919 January 25   League of Nations is founded

1920   United States grants women the right to vote

1921   Airmail service begins in New Zealand

1927   Charles Lindbergh becomes first person to fly across the Atlantic Ocean

1928   New Zealand boxer Edward "Ted" Morgan wins welterweight gold medal at Amsterdam Olympics

1932   U.S. president Franklin D. Roosevelt elected

1939 September 1   World War II begins with Germany's invasion of Poland

1941 December 7   Japanese bomb U.S. fleet at Pearl Harbor in Hawaii

1944 June 6   D-Day invasion of Normandy by Allies

1945   President Franklin D. Roosevelt dies in office

1945   Atomic bomb is dropped on Hiroshima and Nagasaki

1950-1953   The Korean War

1950 June 3   French team climbs Annapurna, at 26,545 feet, the first 26,000+-foot peak to be ascended

1953   Queen Elizabeth is crowned monarch of the United Kingdom

1955   Rosa Parks incites the Montgomery, Alabama bus boycott, a key moment in Civil Rights Movement

1957   Russians launch "Sputnik," starting the space race

Sir Edmund Hillary Timeline (cont.)

1960   Joins search for Abominable Snowman, concluding it is a myth

1962   Appears on television show "What's My Line?" stumping the panel

1967   Part of first group to climb 10,942-foot Mount Herschel in Antarctica

1968   Traverses rivers of Nepal by jet boat

1985-1988   Serves as New Zealand's ambassador to India

1985   Reaches North Pole by airplane, with astronaut Neil Armstrong, becoming first person to climb Everest and reach both Poles

1989   Marries June Mulgrew, a marriage lasting until his death

1992   Image appears on New Zealand five dollar bill

2003   Honorary citizenship bestowed by Nepalese government

2008 January 11   Dies of heart failure in New Zealand.

World Timeline (cont.)

1959   Alaska and Hawaii become the 49th and 50th states in the U.S.

1960   John F. Kennedy is elected U.S. president at age 43

1961   Vietnam War begins as U.S. sends military advisors to Southeast Asia

1963 November 22   President John F. Kennedy is assassinated

1969   Astronaut Neil Armstrong walks on moon

1976 July 4   U.S. celebrates bicentennial of nation

1979   Margaret Thatcher becomes the Prime Minister of the United Kingdom

1986   Space Shuttle Challenger explodes after lift-off

1989   Berlin Wall comes down uniting East and West Germany

1996   Atlanta hosts Summer Olympics

1997 August 31   Diana Princess of Wales is killed in automobile accident

2001 September 11   Terrorist attacks at the World Trade Center

2003   Iraq is invaded in response to terrorism

2005   Hurricane Katrina overpowers Mississippi, Louisiana and Alabama

2007   Recession begins in U.S. and global financial crisis follows

Glossary

British Commonwealth   A voluntary association of 52 countries, most former British colonies, that work together for trade and peace. It contains almost one third of the world's population

Buddhism   A religion and philosophy of life based on the teachings of Buddha

Carabiner   Metal hook shaped in an oblong a few inches in length that can tie climber into a rope for safety or link together equipment so it does not become lost

Crampons   Metal grippers with sharp teeth attached to an outer boot that can dig into snow and ice and allow mountain climbers to step more safely

Crevasse   Dangerous split or crack in ice on a glacier, sometimes unseen as a climber walks along, but can seem almost bottomless viewed from above

Death zone   Human beings at above 26,000 feet (or 8,000 meters) of altitude use more oxygen moving than they can inhale even while resting

Erosion   Gradual destruction by wind, water, or other aspects of nature

Ferguson Tractors   Tractors modified with special tread and fortified against extreme cold, used to cross the Antarctic continent overland

Hinduism   A religious and cultural philosophy home to South Asia

Himalayan Trust   Founded by Edmund Hillary in 1960 benefitting the people of Nepal to build structures and fund educational, cultural, and health opportunities

Himalayas   Mountain range in Asia featuring the world's tallest mountains in India, Pakistan, and China

Ice axe   Metal hiking and climbing tool with a wide handle and a sharp point that can be stabbed into ice or snow to halt a climber's skid or fall

Knighthood   Reward in recognition of great achievement; when the honor is bestowed upon a man in the British Commonwealth, he earns the title "Sir" placed before his name

Mount Everest   Tallest mountain in the world at 29,035-feet (Re-measured in 1999 from 29,029 feet)

North Pole   Northernmost point on earth and place in the Northern Hemisphere where the earth's axis comes together with the surface as a shifting point in the frozen-over Arctic Ocean with the depth of water at nearly 14,000 feet

Pacifist   An individual who is against war and violence

Parka   Thick, heavy outer coat, usually made of a synthetic material, that covers inner layers of clothing and is the best protection against wind and cold a climber wears

Pollination   The process of reproduction of plants, which occurs when pollen is transferred

Sherpa   Ethnic group of people from the countries of Nepal, Bhutan, India, and China, who born and living at high altitude are natural mountain climbers; many of whom are famous for accompanying/aiding Western climbers to summits of the world's tallest peaks

South Pole   Southernmost point on the planet earth, located on the Antarctic continent on the polar ice sheet

Terrain   A section of land, usually used to describe the physical aspects of the land

Bibliography

Douglas, Ed. *Tenzing: Hero of Everest*. Washington D.C.: National Geographic Society Books, 2003.

Fuchs, Sir Vivian and Hillary, Sir Edmund. *The Crossing Of Antarctica*. London, England: Cassell & Company Limited, 1958.

Hillary, Sir Edmund. *Nothing Venture, Nothing Win*. New York: Coward, McCann & Geohegan, Inc., 1975.

Hillary, Sir Edmund. *View From The Summit*. New York: Pocket Books, 1999.

Holzel, Tom and Audrey Salkeld. *First On Everest: The Mystery of Mallory and Irvine*. New York: Paragon House Publishers, 1988.

Hunt, Sir John. *The Conquest Of Everest*. New York: E.P. Dutton & Company, Inc., 1954.

Norgay, Tenzing and James Ramsey Ullman. *Tiger of the Snows: The Autobiography of Tenzing of Everest*. New York: G.P. Putnam's Sons, 1955.

FURTHER READING

Hillary, Edmund. *High Adventure: The True Story of the First Ascent of Everest*. New York: Oxford University Press, 2003.

Johnston, Alexa. *Sir Edmund Hillary: An Extraordinary Life*. New York: Penguin Global, 2005.

Tenzing, Tashi. *Tenzing Norgay and the Sherpas of Everest*. Camden, Maine: International Marine, 2003.

Norgay, Jamling Tenzing and Broughton Coburn. *Touching My Father's Soul*. San Francisco: Harper One, 2001.

Coburn, Broughton. *Triumph on Everest: A Photo Biography of Sir Edmund Hillary*. Washington D.C.: National Geographic Children's Books, 2003.

Index

Also in the All About Series...

All About Amelia Earhart
by Lew Freedman

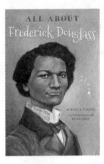

All About Frederick Douglass
by Robin L. Condon

All About Benjamin Franklin
by Elizabeth Zuckerman

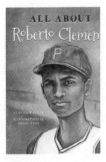

All About Roberto Clemente
by Andrew Conte

And many more!